The Ar 234 flew for the first time on 30 July 1943.

Lightning out of the Blue
The Arado Ar 234

By Manfred Griehl

The world's first jet bomber, the Ar 234, made its first flight on 30 July 1943, more than fifty years ago. It and the other "*Blitzbomber*," the Me 262, were supposed to help repulse the coming Allied invasion in the west.

In October 1941 the *Technische Amt* (Technical Office) of the RLM instructed the Arado company to develop a single-seat reconnaissance aircraft powered by turbojet engines and equipped with a simple skid undercarriage.

Soon afterwards, on 17 April 1942, a contract was issued for six prototypes. On 28 December 1942 the order was increased to twenty prototypes.

On 19 February 1943 a contract was issued for the first two prototypes of a high-speed bomber variant with a retractable undercarriage. Four months later, on 2 June, Arado received an order for twenty of these machines, ten of which were assigned the DE priority level.

Following the first tangible test results, on 10 June 1943 it was proposed that 180, and later 200, of the Ar 234 B production version be built. The delivery plan of 15 August 1943 was the first to include these machines, which were to be delivered between October 1944 and March 1945.

As a result of discussions with *Generalfeldmarschall* Milch concerning the production program, on 19 June 1943 it was decided that at first only the proposed Ar 234 B version would be built, for the bomber and reconnaissance roles. Initial production would concentrate on the B-model, which was powered by two Jumo turbojets; however, at a later date it would be replaced by the C-series with four BMW 003 engines. It was also decided that the aircraft would have a pressurized cockpit. The proposed use of HeS 011 turbojets had to be dropped due to delays in development of that power plant.

The Ar 234 V1 (TG + KB, Werk-Nr. 130001) took to the air for the first time on 30 July 1943 with company test pilot Selle at the controls. In a flight which lasted from 2002 to 2015 hours, Selle examined the type's handling characteristics. An overall assessment was not possible, as the aircraft proved to be very nose-heavy. It did, however, demonstrate adequate stability about all axes. Aileron, rudder, and elevator forces were found to be acceptable.

Rolling moment, trim, and power plants were also judged to be satisfactory. The Ar 234 V1, which took off from a trolley, reached a maximum speed of 650 kph. The takeoff trolley was released at a height of about 500-650 meters with the aircraft climbing out at 230 kph. Unfortunately, both trolleys were wrecked on 30 July 1943 when their parachutes failed to deploy.

The first prototype made its third and last flight on 29 August 1943. Following taxi trials with a new takeoff trolley, the aircraft lifted off at 160 kph. This time the pilot released the trolley immediately. The trolley fell back onto the runway and was stopped by its braking chute in about 150 meters.

Poor weather again prevented a thorough evaluation of the Ar 234, and after about 20 minutes Selle decided to land. He reduced power, lowered the skids as he slowed from 300 and 250 kph, trimmed the machine and applied power again to begin his approach to the company airfield. But then both turbojets quit, and all of Selle's efforts to restart them failed. Unable to reach the airfield, Selle decided to make a forced landing in a small fenced field. The aircraft's tail touched the ground first, reducing its speed. The Arado slid through two fences and came to rest against an overgrown earth wall 160 meters from where it had touched down. The aircraft sustained heavy damage in the forced landing and could not be repaired. The second Ar 234 began flight trials on 13 September 1943, however, on 2 October it was destroyed in a crash near the airfield in which pilot Selle lost his life. Prior to the crash he had reported instrument failure. Observers on the airfield with binoculars saw that the port engine was on fire. The aircraft entered an ever-steepening dive and crashed in a field. Selle had no chance to bail out.

The first flight test reports reached the *Technische Amt* in mid-October 1943. In spite of the loss of the first two aircraft, materials for the construction of a further 500 Ar 234s were approved in Delivery Plan 223.

In keeping with a requirement issued by the *Luftwaffe* General Staff on 23 August, Delivery Plan 225 of 1 December 1943 foresaw a gradual increase in monthly production to 150 jet bombers, however, this output would not be reached until April 1945. In May of that year production would switch to the four-engined Ar 234 C.

A hand-written memo describing the machine's outstanding performance was shown to Hitler at Insterburg on 25 November 1943. The *Führer* was enthusiastic and envisioned the machine as a defensive weapon against an invasion in the west.

As a result of this, Arado director Blume met with GFM Milch on 21 April 1944 and cautiously approached him about being relieved of license production (He 177 and Fw 190) and receiving more personnel for the Ar 234.

As a result of the meeting, Delivery Plan 225/2 of 15 July 1944 called for production of the Ar 234 C-3 to begin in February 1945. The plan did, however, specify a reduction in production numbers for the Ar 234 B in favor of the Ar 234 C, to ensure that production of the C-3 could reach 150 machines per month by July 1945. Another reason for the temporary drop in output was inadequate production capacity, which meant that some of the jigs and tools for the Ar 234 C would have to be obtained by converting those used in the manufacture of the Ar 234 B.

In the early summer of 1944 Director Blume was convinced that license production

Side view of the early Ar E 370 mock-up.

Oblique view of the single-seat Ar E 370 mock-up.

Translated from the German by David Johnston

Copyright © 2001 by Schiffer Publishing, Ltd.

All rights reserved. No part of this work may be reproduced or used in any forms or by any means—graphic, electronic or mechanical, including photocopying or information storage and retrieval systems—without written permission from the copyright holder.

Printed in China.
ISBN: 0-7643-1431-9

This book was originally published under the title,
Arado Ar 234 - Der erste einsatzfähige Strahlbomber der Luftwaffe
by Flugzeug Publikations

We are interested in hearing from authors with book ideas on related topics.

Schiffer Military History
Atglen, PA

Published by Schiffer Publishing Ltd.
4880 Lower Valley Road
Atglen, PA 19310
Phone: (610) 593-1777
FAX: (610) 593-2002
E-mail: Schifferbk@aol.com
Visit our web site at: www.schifferbooks.com
Please write for a free catalog.
This book may be purchased from the publisher.
Please include $3.95 postage.
Try your bookstore first.

In Europe, Schiffer books are distributed by:
Bushwood Books
6 Marksbury Ave.
Kew Gardens
Surrey TW9 4JF
England
Phone: 44 (0) 20 8392-8585
FAX: 44 (0) 20 8392-9876
E-mail: Bushwd@aol.com
Free postage in the UK. Europe: air mail at cost.
Try your bookstore first.

Ar 234 Prototypes

Prototype	Power Plants	WerkNr.	Code	Ready to Fly Date	First Flight	Remarks
Ar 234 V1	2x Jumo 004 A	130001	TG+KB	15-06.1943	30.07.1943	Remarks:
Ar 234 V2	2x Jumo 004 A	130002	DP+AW	27.97.1943	13.09.1943	Destroyed: 29/08/1943
Ar 234 V3	2x Jumo 004 A	130003	DP+AX	25.08.1943	29.09.1943	Destroyed: 02/10/1943
Ar 234 V4	2x Jumo 004 A	130004	DP+AY	15.09.1943	26.11.1943	Retired: August 1944
Ar 234 V5	2x Jumo 004 A	130005	GK+IV	20-10.1943	22.12.1944	Retired: August 1944
Ar 234 V6	4x BMW 003 A	130006	GK+IW	08.04.1944	25.04.1944	Destroyed: 28/08/1944
Ar 234 V7	2x Jumo 004 B	130007	GK+IX	20-06.1944	22.06.1944	Destroyed: 01/06/1944
Ar 234 V8	4x BMW 003 A	130008	GK+IY	01-02.1944	04.02.1944	Retired: 19/11/1944
Ar 234 V9	2x Jumo 004 B	130009	PH+SQ	10.03.1944	12.03.1944	Destroyed: 06/05/1944
Ar 234 V10	2x Jumo 004 B	130010	PH+SR	02.04.1944	07.04.1944	On strength: December 1944
Ar 234 VI I	2x Jumo 004 B	130011	PH+SS	05-05.1944	10.05.1944	Destroyed: 22/07/1944
Ar 234 V12	2x Jumo 004 B	130022	PH+ST	01.09.1944	14.09.1944	Ready to fly: March 1945
Ar 234 V13	4x BMW 003 A-1	130023	PH+SU	30.08.1944	06.09.1944	Destroyed: 04/04/1945
Ar 234 V14	2x Jumo 004 B	130024	PH+SV	15.10.1944	Dez. 1944	Destroyed: 06/09/1944
Ar 234 V15	4x BMW 003 A-1	130025	PH+SW	10.07.1944	20.07.1944	Blown up: April 1945
Ar 234 V16	2x BMW 003 TLR	130026	-----	05.01.1944	---	Destroyed: April 1945
Ar 234 V17	2x BMW 003 A-1	130027	PI+SY	15.09.1944	25.09.1944	Destroyed: May 1945
Ar 234 V18	4x BMW 003 A-1	130028	-----	15-02.1945	08.03.1945	Destroyed:04/04/1945
Ar 234 V19	4x BMW 003 A-1	130029	PI+WX	30.09.1944	16.10.1944	On strength: April 1945
Ar 234 V20	4x BMW 003 A-1	130030	PI+WY	10.10.1944	05.11.1944	Blown up: April 1945
Ar 234 V21	4x BMW 003 A-1	130061	Pf+WZ	15.11.1944	24.11.1944	Destroyed: 04/04/1945
Ar 234 V22	4x BMW 003 A-1	130062	RK+EL	01.12.1944	01.01.1945	On strength: February 1945
Ar 234 V23	4x BMW 003 A-1	130063	RK+EM	15.12.1944	14.01.1945	On strength: April 1945
Ar 234 V24	4x BMW 003 A-1	130064	RK+EN	31.12.1944	12.01.1945	On strength: March 1945
Ar 234 V25	4x BMW 003 A-1	130065	RK+EO	25.01.1945	02.02.1945	On strength: March 1945
Ar 234 V26	4x BMW 003 A-1	130066	-----	10.02.1945	-----	Blown up: 02/05/1945
Ar 234 V27	4x BMW 003 A-1	-----	-----	28.02.1945	-----	Experimental Wing III – Trials
Ar 234 V28	4x BMW 003 A-1	-----	-----	10.03.1945	-----	Night Fighter Ar 234 C-3/N
Ar 234 V29	4x BMW 003 A-1	-----	-----	20.03.1945	-----	Command aircraft Ar 234 C-5
Ar 234 V30	4x BMW 003 A-1	-----	-----	30.03.1945	-----	Command aircraft Ar 234 C-5
Ar 234 V31	4x BMW 003 A-1	-----	-----	05.05.1945	-----	Laminar Wing III – Trials
Ar 234 V32	4x BMW 003 A-1	-----	-----	15.07.1945	-----	Experimental Wing IV – Trials
Ar 234 V33	2x HeS O11 A-1	-----	-----	15.08.1945	-----	Experimental Wing IV – Trials
Ar 234 V34	2x HeS O11 A-1	-----	-----	01-09.1945	-----	Bomber Ar 234 D-1
Ar 234 V35	2x HeS O11 A-1	-----	-----	20.09.1945	-----	Night Fighter Ar 234 D-2
Ar 234 V36	2x HeS O11 A-1	-----	-----	10-10.1945	-----	Close-Support Aircraft Ar 234 D-3
Ar 234 V37	2x HeS O11 A-1	-----	-----	01-11.1945	-----	Bomber Ar 234 D-1
Ar 234 V38	2x HeS O11 A-1	-----	-----	20.11.1945	-----	Night Fighter Ar 234 D-2
Ar 234 V39	2x HeS O11 A-1	-----	-----	10.12.1945	-----	Close-Support Aircraft Ar 234 D-3
Ar 234 V40	2x HeS O11 A-1	-----	-----	31.12.1945	-----	Bomber Ar 234 D-1

The Ar 234 V6, seen here, was lost in a crash on its seventh flight on 1 June 1944. The machine was identical to the Ar 234 V7 (T9 + MH) long-range reconnaissance aircraft.

The Ar 234 V8 photographed during takeoff.

of the He 177 would have to be terminated if production of the Ar 234 was to be accelerated. The end of heavy bomber production brought some short-term relief, however, production of the Fw 190 still proved a hindrance to the progress of the Ar 234 production program.

Meanwhile, revised plans called for the maximum monthly production to be raised from 150 to 500 aircraft. The majority of the new construction aircraft were to be from the Ar 234 C series, which, it was calculated, would surpass the Ar 234 B-2 in speed and altitude performance. Furthermore, the C-3 would be capable of carrying either one 1,000-kg or three 400-kg stores, compared to one 500-kg bomb or bomb-dispenser by the Ar 234 B. In addition, the use of four BMW 003 turbojets would free more Jumo 004s for production of the Me 262 A-1a.

The BMW company declared unequivocally that its turbojet engines were already sufficiently reliable, and that output was sufficient to provide adequate numbers for the first two months of Ar 234 C production. From an early date, however, Director Blume expressed the view that the technical problems with the BMW 003 had not yet been resolved. In his view the test base for the BMW 003 was very narrow, and furthermore had been delayed in recent months. Since the jigs for production of the Ar 234 C had been converted from those for the Ar 234 B, the option of initially continuing production of the Ar 234 B powered by two Jumo 004s was not available.

All of the prototypes up to the Ar 234 V8 were built with a skid undercarriage. The complicated takeoff procedure proved a disadvantage, and a fully-retractable undercarriage was developed.

The first Ar 234 equipped with a retractable undercarriage (Ar 234 V9, Werk-Nr. 130009, PH + SQ) made its maiden flight on 12 March 1944. It also served as a transfer flight for the prototype to Alt-Lönnewitz. This machine made more than 110 flights, however, its ultimate fate is not known. The last known flight by the V9 took place on 2 December 1944 with Arado pilot Eheim at the controls.

By 7 April 1944 the second prototype equipped with a conventional undercarriage, the Ar 234 V10, was ready to fly, and was likewise ferried to Alt-Lönnewitz.

The first "Zero-Series" (pre-production) aircraft (beginning with Werk-Nr. 140101, GM + BA) became available in June 1944. Most were delivered to the *Erprobungskommando Lärz (234)*.

On 10 June 1944 *III./Kampfgesch-wader 65*, which was scheduled to convert to the jet bomber, was transferred to the Arado factories to gain on the spot information and experience with the new type. This also had the advantages of providing support for the factory during construction and reducing the time required to train the technical personnel and test the machines. Deliveries of production aircraft began with five machines in July 1944 and ten in August. A further 18 jet bombers were delivered in September 1944, and 40 in both October and November. At this time the Ar 234 was called the "*Hechte*" (Pike) as per a "*Führer* Directive" (Suggestive Names for Weapons). In December 1944 output fell to 35 aircraft, while just 15 were built in February 1945 due to the effects of the war.

At the beginning of October 1944 testing of the equipment necessary for the bombing role was still incomplete. On 2 October the Operations Staff ordered the Ar 234 B-2 into action with interim equipment and an intensification of flight training. In the beginning bombing accuracy was on a par with results achieved by the Me 262 A-1a/Bo and the Me 262 A-2a.

The *Kommodore* of *Kampfgesch-wader 76*, *Oberst* Storp, was ordered to have at least one *Staffel* ready for operations by 15 November 1944, however, numerous technical problems were encountered, not all of which could be rectified. One modification involved the installation of Teves pumps to increase braking power and allow the machine to land on relatively short fields. As the war situation deteriorated, more of the long runways at Germany's permanent airfields were put out of action by the Allies. A braking parachute was also installed, reducing the aircraft's landing roll by 500 to 600 meters. The installation of the braking chute took place in the Grossenhain conversion facility, which required just six days to convert an Ar 234 after it left the production line.

As a result of tactical trials, a statoscope was added to the Lotfe bombsight, and the pilot was provided with a rearwards-facing periscope to better enable him to detect threats from the rear. All in all, these modifications, which were adopted on the production line, resulted in a much improved Ar 234. Most importantly, the Arado was soon achieving better bombing results than the Me 262 "*Blitzbomber*," which lacked a bombsight for accurate bombing.

By 15 November 1944 sixteen aircraft had been modified with all these changes and could be reported operational. At that time, pilots involved in the flight trials at Rechlin began encountering elevator vibration and aileron and nosewheel problems. For flight safety reasons, therefore, the Test Stations Command (KdE) requested that all Ar 234s be grounded. The grounding lasted from 24 to 30 November 1944. As the problems were eliminated, restrictions were lifted on the aircraft, which could be

Ar 234s of III./KG 76 at Alt-Lönnewitz.

One of the two 109-500 takeoff assist rockets, the so-called "smoke dischargers".

dived safely at speeds up to 850 kph with up to 2.5 g pull-outs.

The aircraft of *1. Staffel* of III./KG 76 were the first to receive the necessary modifications, after which the *Kommodore* reported the unit operational.

At that time service aircraft were capable of 712 kph at full thrust with external bomb load and 742 kph clean at an altitude of 6,000 m. These figures exceeded test results achieved in the summer of 1944, however, it must be taken into account that by winter an increase in engine performance had resulted in a speed increase of up to 50 kph.

A survey from the beginning of January 1945 listed 116 machines which had been manufactured by 16 December 1944. Seven of these had already been written off and ten were under repair. The *Kommando der E-Stelle* had on strength eleven test machines, which are listed below.

140102 Testing of statoscope with bomb-sight
140105 Jumo 004 engine tests
140106 Simplified statoscope switch and PDS system
140107 Diving tests, performance and winter ranges
140108 Handling quality measurements and undercarriage endurance trials
140109 *Deichselschlepp* ("air trailer") and FuG 203 and Hs 293 (drops planned)
140110 High-speed braking chute, tests with Hs 293 planned
140111 Radio trials: FuG 217, 136, 102 and new antenna FuG 16 ZY
140113 Written off during delivery
140117 Written off
140145 "*Nachtigall*" night fighter
140150 Trials with TSA 2D system
140343 High-speed stores release

On 18 February 1945 the survivors were joined by several more machines:

140102 Installation of second camera
140105 Engine trials: Jumo 004 with new valves
140106 Simplified statoscope switch, high-altitude flights planned
140107 Readied for operations
140109 Operational as bomber on 14 February 1945
140110 Bomb-aiming equipment in installation
140111 Continuation of radio trials
140114 Installation of solid-fuel takeoff-assist rockets
140150 Readied for operations
140160 Readied for operations
140343 Readied for operations

The Ar 234 B-2s of the *E-Stelle Rechlin* assigned to operations were to be committed on the Eastern Front as part of a *Gefechtsverband* (battle unit), which included available Ta 152s, Fw 190s, Ju 88s, and other types. Two other aircraft, including Werk-Nr. 140152, were used by Arado as company aircraft for test purposes.

In addition to three "interim night fighters," nineteen aircraft were planned as reconnaissance machines. Of these four were already in service and fifteen were undergoing conversion. The majority of Ar 234s were with KG 76, which had nine machines for operational training alone. On 10 December 1944 the unit had twenty aircraft available for combat missions. Three more Ar 234 B-2s were received by 17 December, another 13 by 24 December, and 19 more by the end of the year.

The company calculated that 150 machines would be produced by 31 December

Ar 234 B under tow behind an Opel Blitz fuel truck.

1944, a further 35 in January, and the remaining 25 of the Ar 234 B series on schedule by February. Thus, the first production series would have totaled 210 machines.

In fact, however, 188 machines were delivered by 20 February 1945. At the beginning of 1945 production began breaking down because of the catastrophic transportation situation. Just fifteen more aircraft were expected to be completed in March 1945.

The *E-Stelle Rechlin* had begun receiving the first five production aircraft on 7 July 1944. At the Rechlin-Lärz airfield, just a few kilometers away, formation of a test detachment from KG 76 began on 10 July. The detachment was commanded by *Oberleutnant* Spadiut.

As the *E-Stelle* was hopelessly overburdened with its many test programs, on occasion the test detachment had to be brought in to assist with the technical testing of the Arado. This was especially true of the radio and bomb-aiming equipment.

On 31 October 1944 the test detachment moved to Burg bei Magdeburg, where it concentrated on the installation of the braking parachute and the bomb-aiming system. Not until 15 December 1944 was the test detachment disbanded, and further trials were concentrated at Rechlin. From October 1944, purely tactical service trials were carried out by the test *Staffel* (*Kommando Lukesch*) with ten to twelve aircraft. This had been preceded by an order from the *Reichsmarschall* that the Ar 234 B-2 was to go into action in the west as soon as possible with a payload of one 500-kg bomb. As a result, the delivery of nine aircraft was accelerated.

In the period from 1 to 30 November 1944 the number of available aircraft on strength with KG 76 rose from 48 to 54, and these logged approximately 85 hours in the air. Tests revealed an endurance of barely 80 minutes when carrying 2,800 liters of J2 fuel and an average speed of 700 kph.

On 10 November 1944 an advance detachment went to Münster-Handorf. The ground elements of 9./KG 76 (Hptm. Lukesch) arrived by vehicle two days later.

On 30 November 1944 KG 76 had a total of 68 Ar 234 B-2s on strength. One machine was assigned to the *Geschwaderstab*, *III. Gruppe* had 51 bombers, and the *Einsatzstaffel Lukesch* (operational *Staffel*) 16. In spite of several tragic accidents, testing of the new type proceeded rapidly. On 1 December 1944 *Major* Bätcher assumed command of *III. Gruppe*. In mid-December, after sufficient Ar 234 Bs had been delivered, the OKL decided to form a second operational *Staffel*. As well, *III. Gruppe* was to form a third Arado *Staffel* as quickly as possible.

The operational *Staffel*, which had been transferred to Handorf, was finally declared operational in mid-December. At that time the unit had 16 officers and 223 men plus ten Ar 234s. Other aircraft were in Burg awaiting delivery to the unit. Oblt. Stark acted as Hptm. Lukesch's deputy, while Oblt. Saß was technical officer. Beginning on 22 December 1944 the operational *Staffel* received its mission orders from KG 51 *"Edelweiß."* Poor weather hampered operations, however, on 24 December nine Ar 234 B-2s took off on the first combat mission. The first jet bomber took off at 1014 hours, and within twelve minutes all nine were airborne. Between 1050 and 1100 hours the bombers hit railway installations and factories in Liège and Namur, attacking in a shallow dive from 2,000 meters. The aircraft returned from the mission between 1122 and 1148 hours. Two hits were scored on the center of the track system, one on a large complex of buildings in the center of Liège, and one on a factory.

On returning to base, Uffz. Winguth found that the nosewheel of his aircraft (F1 + PT) would not lower, and the aircraft sustained minor damage in the ensuing landing. The pilot escaped injury.

A second mission was flown later that same day by eight aircraft. At about 1600 hours the pilots set course for Liège's northern railway station. Again they approached in a shallow dive and released their bombs. The bomb became hung up on one of the Ar 234 B-2s, and its pilot made a risky landing at Handorf with the load still in place. In addition, the pilots also visually reconnoitered the rail yards in Liège. Hptm. Lukesch's aircraft was slightly damaged on landing as a result of an undercarriage fault.

By 24 January 1945 the *Einsatzstaffel Lukesch* flew a total of 16 missions, mainly against targets in and around Antwerp, Brussels, Liège, and Namur, as well as during the Ardennes offensive. The pilots normally attacked the assigned target in loose formation. A controversy developed between the *Luftwaffe* Commander-in-Chief and the *General der Kampfflieger* (commanding general bombers) concerning tactical mission requirements. Göring demanded surprise attacks on targets in the enemy's rear areas in order to split the Allied air defenses. The *General der Kampfflieger* saw this as inefficient and instead called for the use of a unit of 30 Ar 234 Bs against a single target. On 31 December 1944 the operational *Staffel* left KG 51's area of command.

By this time KG 76 had 53 Ar 234s. Four machines had crashed in the period 23 to 31 December 1944 as a result of technical defects and pilot error. The conversion of additional pilots also led to several crashes and the loss of pilots and machines.

On 11 January 1945, *III. Gruppe*, which had still not completed its conversion training, was ordered to Achmer. At the same time, II./KG 76 was experiencing problems converting to the jet bomber, mainly because of a lack of aircraft.

Beginning on 12 February 1945, additional elements of *III. Gruppe* began taking an active part in the fighting in the northwest. As a rule the bombers attacked in a shallow dive from 4,000 to 2,000 meters, releasing their bombs between 2,000 and 1,500 meters. The normal bomb load consisted of one SC 500, SD 500, or one AB 500 bomb dispenser loaded with SD 15 anti-personnel bombs. The majority of targets were in the Kleve-Eindhoven area, or in Aachen, Brussels, Mönchengladbach, or Maastricht.

On 7 March 1945 the American 9th Armored Division reached the Rhine near Remagen and seized the Ludendorff Bridge before the demolition charges were set off. The Americans immediately began massing light and medium anti-aircraft guns around the bridge and in the bridgehead. The OKL ordered all available assets committed to destroy the bridge. Attacks were flown against the bridge by the *Blitzbombers* (Me 262s) of KG 51, close-support aircraft, dive bombers, and the Ar 234s of KG 76. A *"Zerstörer"* (destroyer) attack by three Ar 234s on 9 March failed. Göring's call for a suicide mission to take out the bridge went unanswered by KG 76. When Hitler also spoke out against such a mission, the idea was dropped, and instead further diving attacks were planned. These took place between 11 and 17 March. Approximately 50 to 60 Ar 234s attacked the Ludendorff Bridge, inflicting such damage that it collapsed a short time later. In the meantime, however, American engineers had erected several pontoon bridges, allowing the bridgehead on the east bank of the Rhine to be supplied.

After the Remagen attacks, the bombers returned to targets in western Germany and Belgium. On 19 March four jet bombers of 6./KG 76 attacked the marshalling yards in Brussels. At the same time, fragmentation bombs were dropped on an airfield east of Brussels.

In front of the hangar: the Ar 234 V6 and the Ar 234 V8 (right).

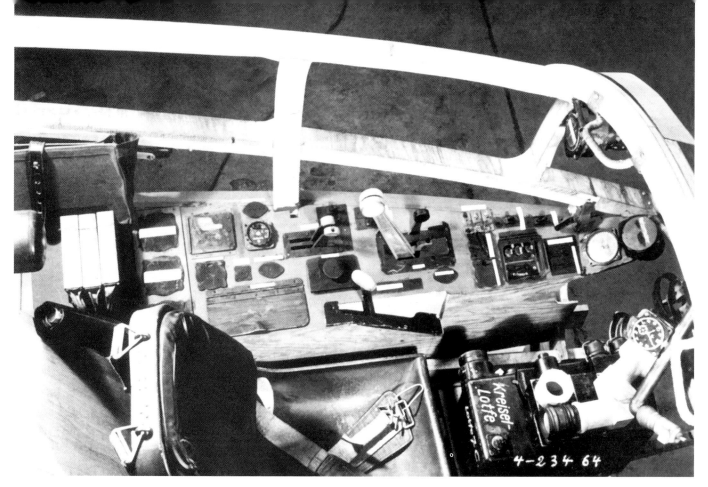

Ar 234 cockpit mock-up, port console.

Pilot seat and starboard console of the Ar 234 B (mock-up).

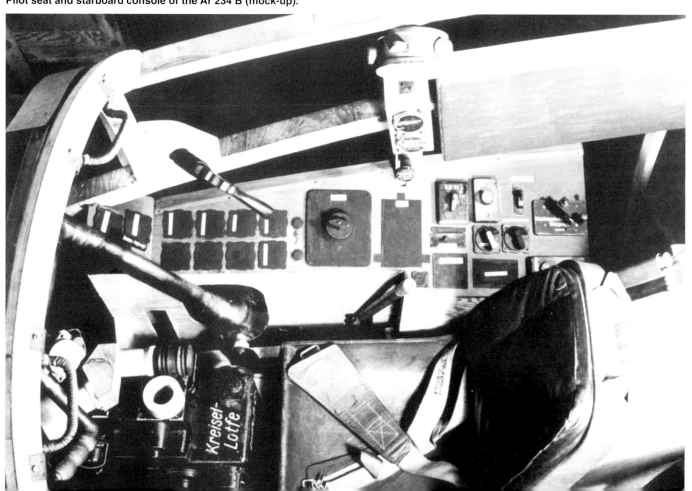

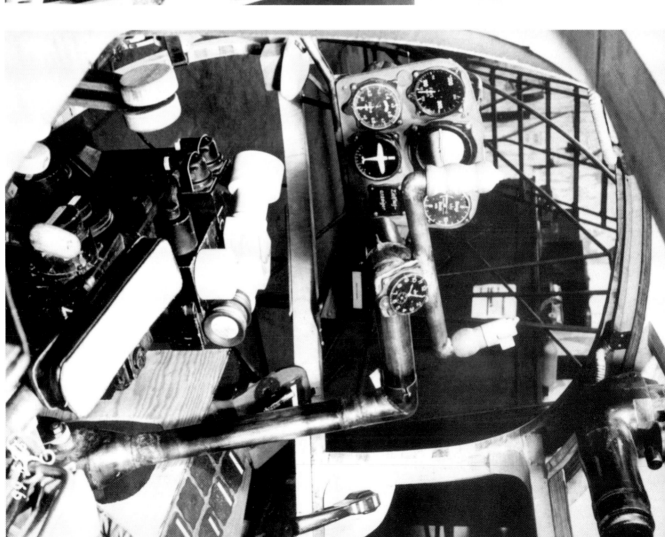

Ar 234 B cockpit mock-up.

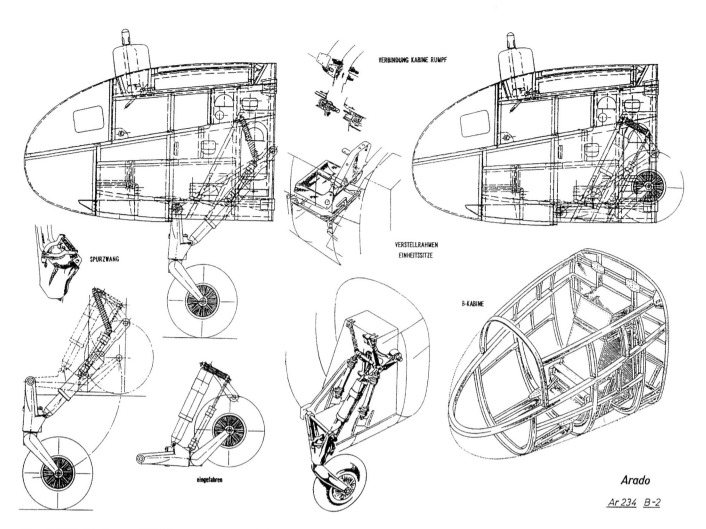

Front view of the Ar 234 V1 (TG + KB).

Improved cockpit mock-up.

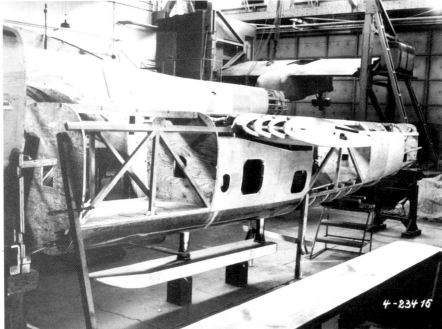

Ar 234 fuselage mock-up.

Comparative views of the Ar 234 A ...

and the Ar 234 B.

The Ar 234 V9 was nearly identical to the ultimate high-speed bomber version.

Side view of the ninth prototype with bomb racks beneath its two turbojet engines.

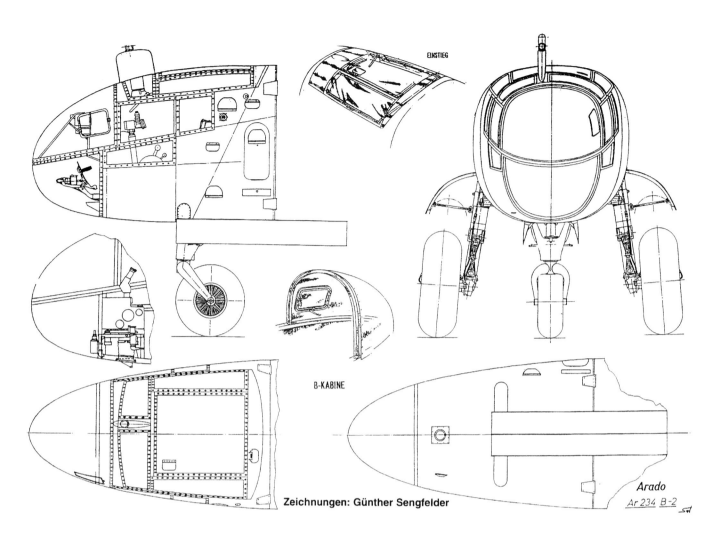

Zeichnungen: Günther Sengfelder

Arado Ar 234 B-2

Front view of the new prototype during factory trials.

Ar 234 – Operations with KG 76

Date	Number of Aircraft	Remarks
24/12/1944	8	Railway and factory targets Liège and Namur area
	8	Liège north station
25/12/1944	8	Railway and factory targets Liège area
	8	Railway and factory targets area northwest of Liège
26/12/1944	6	Troop movements in Verviers area and east of Liège
	6	Targets in area of Libramont station, southwest of Bastogne
27/12/1944	5	Troop movements near Neufchateau, south of Bastogne
	8	Troop concentration south of Bastogne
31/12/1944	10	Troops in Bastogne pocket
31/12/1944/ 01/01/1945	4	Night mission: weather reconnaissance over southern England, Belgium, Lower Rhine and harassing attack on Brussels North station
	6	Air attack on Gilze-Rijen airfield with six AB 500 bomb dispensers
01/01/1945/ 02/01/1945	4	Night mission against port of Antwerp and railway targets in Brussels
	5	Night mission against troop movements and rail installations in the Mechelen—Loeven—Brussels area, including main Brussels station.
14/01/1945	5	Troop movements near Bastogne with AB 500 dispensers
20/01/1945	8	Shipping targets in port of Antwerp
24/01/1945	4	Shipping targets and depots in port of Antwerp
08/02/1945	7	Brussels marshalling yards
14/02/1945	16	Troop movements in area around Kleve and Eindhoven
	16	Troop movements in Kleve area
21/02/1945	21	Troop movements in the Kleve—Bedburg—Eindhoven area
	16	Troop movements near Kleve and the area of Eindhoven, Reichswald
22/02/1945	9	Troop assembly areas approx. 20 km southeast and northeast of Aachen
	14	Troop concentration east of Aachen
25/02/1945	10	Troop concentration 25 km northeast of Aachen
02/03/1945	2	Bombed troop movements in area south of Mönchengladbach—Jülich—Aachen—Maastricht (1st mission by Stab KG 76)
03/03/1945	1	Weather reconnaissance and harassment attack
09/03/1945	3	Attack on Remagen bridge, III./KG 76
11/03/1945	2	Attack on Remagen bridge, III./KG 76
12/03/1945	2	Attack on Remagen bridge, Stab KG 76
	2	Attack on Remagen bridge, 6./KG 76
	14	Attack on Remagen bridge by remaining forces of III./KG 76, blind bombing with SC 1000 with Egon control
13/03/1945	7	Attack on Remagen bridge (no bombs dropped due to weather)
	12	Attack on Remagen bridge
14/03/1945	11	Attack on Remagen bridge
	8	Attack on installations in port of Antwerp and targets in Liège area
17/03/1945	2	Harassment attack on Remagen bridgehead with AB 500 (filled with SD 15)
19/03/1945	4	Attack on airfield east of Brussels and Brussels marshalling yards
	3	Armor concentration near Bad Kreuznach
	2	Armor concentration near Bad Kreuznach
	9	Rail installations in Brussels area
20/03/1945	4	Armor assembly area 4 km northeast of Bad Kreuznach and flak position
21/03/1945	4	Armor assembly area northeast of Bad Kreuznach and flak position
29/03/1945	5	Armor assembly area between Sobernheim and Bad Kreuznach
30/03/1945	2	Armed reconnaissance in Arnhem – Wesel area
01/04/1945	10	Troop movements in the Münster—Osnabrück area
02/04/1945	6	Vehicle concentration 10 km southeast of Rheine (with SC 250 and AB 500)
	1	Armed reconnaissance in Arnhem – Wesel area
03/04/1945	3	Troop concentration in area east of Wesel
	8	Various targets in northern Germany
04/04/1945	3	Vehicle columns in Nordhorn area and northwest of Rheine
	4	Targets in Münster area (III./KG 76)
05/04/1945	8	Armor concentration in Lembruck area northeast of Osnabrück and armor assembly area near Bohmte 06/04/1945
	6	Armor concentration west of Achmer (by III./KG 76)
	5	Horizontal attack on vehicles near Bohmte northeast of Osnabrück
07/04/1945	3	Canal bridge near Vinte southwest of Achmer (by III./KG 76)
09/04/1945	2	Targets in northwestern Germany
10/04/1945	2	Vehicle columns on the Reichsautobahn between Bad Oeynhausen and Hanover
11/04/1944	5	Artillery positions near Kirchweihe
12/04/1945	3	Artillery positions near Kirchweihe
13/04/1945	2	Bridgehead on the Aller near Essel
14/04/1945	5	Aller bridgehead, 25 km northeast of Celle, and vehicle columns on the Reichsautobahn between Hanover and Brunswick
15/04/1945	3	Targets on the Reichsautobahn between Hanover and Brunswick and troop concentrations
18/04/1945	1	Weather reconnaissance in area of Aller bridges near Rethen
19/04/1945	1	Enemy tanks south of Berlin
	1	Bridge target near Rethen (one SD 500)
20/04/1945	1	Tank traffic jam on the Zossen—Baruth road south of Berlin
23/04/1945	3	Armed reconnaissance and attacks on bridge targets in Berlin area
25/04/1945	3	Bridge targets in the Berlin area
26/04/1945	3	Tanks in metropolitan Berlin
27/04/1945	2	Harassing attack in Berlin area (Stab KG 76)
29/04/1945	2	Harassing attack in Berlin area (Stab KG 76)
	2	Armor columns in Berlin area
30/04/1945	2	Targets in government quarter in Berlin
02/05/1945	2	Vehicle column on the Reichsautobahn near Lübeck
03/05/1945	2	Vehicle assembly area south of Bremervörde

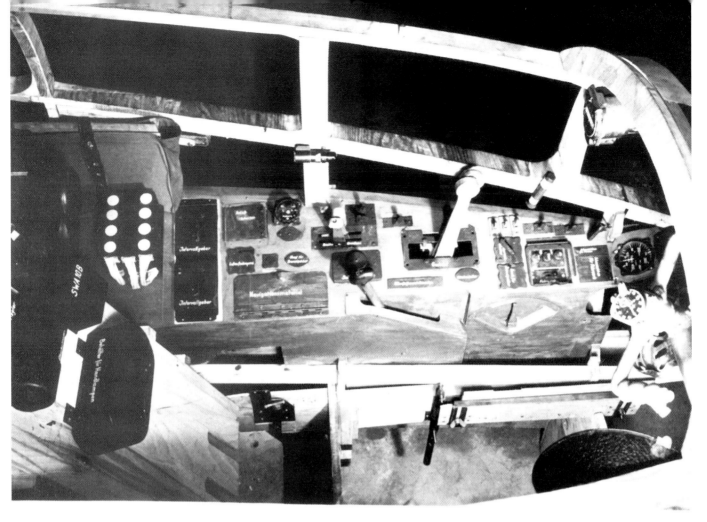

Slightly modified cockpit arrangement of the Ar 234 B (mock-up).

The mock-up illustrates the cramped nature of the single-seat cockpit.

During this raid the Arados were attacked by RAF Spitfires.

On 21 March the Arados bombed Allied concentration areas north of Bad Kreuznach. Some of the aircraft which made the attack sustained considerable damage, however all returned safely to Hesepe.

As a result of the Allied advance, KG 76 was forced to pull back into the Wilhelmshaven area. At the beginning of April 1945 the *Stab* KG 76 had just two aircraft, while *6. Staffel* had four Ar 234s and *8.* and *9. Staffel* had a total of eleven bombers between them. Meanwhile, elements of *II. Gruppe* moved to Burg, from where some of the unit's personnel assisted the manufacturer. The handful of operational aircraft attacked concentrations of enemy armor in northern Germany. Missions were also flown from Lübeck-Blankensee and Kaltenkirchen against bridges over the Aller and in the Berlin area.

Beginning on 21 April 1945 the *Stab* and the *I.* and *III. Gruppe* of KG 76 were reunited in Kaltenkirchen near Hamburg. Five days later, when Obfw. Breme flew his Ar 234 B-2 over embattled Berlin, he was able to make out Russian tanks in the city. The *Geschwader* flew a number of sorties over Berlin on 29 and 30 April, including eight by the *Kommodore* alone. The fuel shortage caused the number of missions to drop drastically. What was probably the last offensive mission was flown on 3 May 1945, when Obfw. Drewes attacked Allied vehicles near Bremerförde. The surrender came soon afterward.

The first four Ar 234 C-3s arrived on 3 May 1945, too late for operational use. On 5 May the last nine serviceable Ar 234 B-2s took off for Stavanger, Norway, under the command of Oblt. Kolm. All unserviceable machines were blown up in Leck.

The *Geschwader* was interned on 9 May 1945. Most members of the *Geschwader* were released by mid-July 1945.

The Arado Ar 234 C

The first prototype to largely resemble the planned C production version made its maiden flight on 16 October 1944. The first Ar 234 C completed factory trials at the end of December 1944, and the pilots described its handling qualities as superior to those of the Ar 234 B-2.

The second report by the KdE's specialist department, Fl-E 2 submitted on 21 December 1944, revealed that quantity production could begin in the summer of 1945, provided sufficient jigs and tools were available. By autumn 1944, however, the constant air attacks and the steadily worsening situation made it appear unlikely that a two-seat version of the Ar 234 would be introduced.

The much-requested two-man cockpit was inspected by representatives of the RLM and the KdE on 30 October 1944 and received general approval.

The Ar 234 V21, which featured a revised cockpit, flew for the first time on 24 November 1944.

The situation report by the Chef TLR Fl-E 2 dated 21 February 1945 dealt with the Me 262, Ta 152, He 162, Do 335, and the Ar 234 C:

"Based on combat experience to date, the Ar 234 B can continue to operate with success. While the Ar 234 C achieves significantly higher speeds, in unit service considerable difficulties can be expected with the four jet engines in the area of operational readiness.

When the E-Stelle examined the Ar 234 C-3 it was found that the expanded radio equipment could not be installed in such a way that the pilot could operate all the systems.

Front-line experience has also shown that, given the short mission times, assembling into formation is not possible on account of enemy fighter defenses and fuel consumption. Use of the Lotfe sight (horizontal bombing) is therefore not practical. The aircraft bomb with the BZA or the low-altitude bombing system (TSA)."

The author of the report proposed that the Ar 234 B-2 be kept in production as a temporary measure pending the resolution of the Ar 234 C-3's problems, especially since the Jumo 004 engines used by the former would soon be fitted with afterburners, resulting in a thrust increase of 1,150 to 1,200 kg of thrust. The more powerful engines would give the Ar 234 B-2 a significantly higher maximum speed. An alternative proposal for a more potent replacement called for a switch to a version of the Ar 234 C powered by two HeS 011 engines at the earliest possible date.

At the beginning of 1945 the *Kommando der Erprobungsstellen* and the OKL were confident that February's target of three Ar 234 C-3s could be met, and that conversion of the BMW 003 from B4 to J2 fuel could be accomplished in a relatively short time.

However, Germany's collapsing infrastructure made it virtually impossible to procure enough engines and fuel for the first series, the Ar 234 B-2.

Future plans called for the BZA 1B to be installed in the first fifty examples of the Ar 234 C-3. Installation of the TSA IIB system was not possible after the fifteenth C-3 as the necessary installation documents had not arrived. It was therefore decided that the BZA 1B system would be replaced by the TSA IID bombsight beginning with the 51st Ar 234 C-3.

Because of the drastically worsening military situation, on 12 March 1945 the OKL-Chef TLR suspended further development of the Ar 234 C. From that date Department E2, which was responsible for airframe development, would concern itself only with the Me 262 C-1a and C-2b home defense fighters and the

The V20, which was destroyed in Wesendorf on 4 April 1945.

Ho 229 within the framework of the "*Führer* Emergency Program."

The first Ar 234 C-3 aircraft to reach KG 76 at the beginning of May 1945 were too late to see action.

Ar 234 Reconnaissance Aircraft

The Ar 234 was also built for the reconnaissance role. Several prototypes were converted into interim reconnaissance machines and were employed in the west. This was followed by the conversion of B-2 production aircraft for the high-speed reconnaissance role over western Europe through the installation of two cameras.

These conversions, which were the result of a request by the *General der Aufklärungsflieger* (GdA), did nothing to hamper the production program, as no major airframe changes were required. Strictly speaking, the use of the Ar 234 in the reconnaissance role can be traced back to a directive from Adolf Hitler, who, after a presentation by *Generaloberst* Jodl, bemoaned the *Luftwaffe*'s inability to mount effective reconnaissance missions over western Europe and southern England.

On 23 May 1944, therefore, the OKL-Gen QU. 2 Abt. (IIa) ordered the immediate reorganization of the OKL test unit (*Versuchsverband OKL*) into three *Staffeln*. The first of these, com-

Layout of the navigational instruments and engine gauges in the cockpit of the Ar 234 B (mock-up).

Close-up of the cockpit mock-up with circuit breakers and engine gauges.

Ar 234 C cockpit mock-up.

Mock-up of the fixed armament of the Ar 234 C.

T9 + KH, an Ar 234 B, is towed to the runway in preparation for takeoff.

T9 + HH, an aircraft of Kommando Sommer, is pushed into a well-camouflaged hangar.

Mock-up of the first two-seat version of the Ar 234 C series.

Rearward the rear of the two-seat cockpit mock-up.

manded by Hptm. Götz, was to form three operational detachments (*Einsatzkommandos*):

Kommando Götz (later *Kommando Sperling*)
Kommando Hecht (later *Kommando Sommer*)
Kommando Braunegg (Me 262 reconnaissance aircraft)

As a result of this, the 1./Vers. ObdL was placed under the direct operational command of the *General der Aufklärungsflieger*. These numerically small operational detachments allowed the *Luftwaffe* to resume reconnaissance missions over the west on a modest scale, and the high-speed machines were able to operate without loss to themselves.

In March 1945 Kommando Sperling was combined with 1. (F)/123 under the command of *Major* Götz, and in April was disbanded at Hohn air base. *Kommando Hecht* became part of 1. (F)/100 at Biblis and was disbanded there at the beginning of April 1945. Oblt. Sommer formed *Kommando Sommer* in Udine, Italy, in March 1945. The unit met its end in Heiligenkreuz, Bavaria, in May 1945. By the beginning of May all that was left of the operational aircraft was the charred remains of two Ar 234 B-1s at Campo Formido. The fate of the third Ar 234 used in Italy is not known.

In January 1945 the 1. (F)/123 commanded by Hptm. Hattan was equipped with Ar 234 reconnaissance aircraft. 1./FAGr. 5 received its first Ar 234 B-1 turbojet reconnaissance aircraft at the beginning of 1945 and was last stationed in Stavanger, Norway. The unit conducted its final reconnaissance mission, over port facilities on the east coast of England, on 10 April 1945.

All of the reconnaissance machines used by the previously-mentioned units retained their bomb racks, bomb release circuitry, and bomb sights. Conversion for the reconnaissance role involved the installation of two cameras by personnel of the GdA.

Each conversion required 700 man-hours of work and took approximately ten days. The necessary equipment sets (Rüstsätze) were always available in sufficient numbers.

Conversion Detachment A (*Umrüstkommando A*) converted a total of eleven Ar 234 reconnaissance machines in February 1945.

On 28 April 1945 the majority of Ar 234 reconnaissance machines were in the hands of the following *Luftwaffe* units:

Kdo. Sommer — *Luftwaffe* Commanding General in Italy
1. (F)/123 — *Luftwaffe* Commanding General in Denmark
1. (F)/100 — 7. Jagddivision (7th Fighter Division)
1. (F)/123 — 14. Fliegerdivision (14th Air Division)

In addition, aircraft of KG 76, last under the command of the *14. Fliegerdivision*, were also used for weather reconnaissance and visual reconnaissance missions.

When the war ended, advancing Allied forces captured six Ar 234s at Grove (Karup, Denmark), and one damaged Ar 234 was found near Bad Wörrishofen. As well, in the final days of the war a number of aircraft were flown to Stavanger in Norway. The remnants of 1. (F)/100, which on 26 April 1945 had just one serviceable Ar 234, was forced to withdraw to Hörsching near Linz. Other Ar 234s of KG 76, most of them wrecked, were found by British troops at Leck and Lübeck-Blankensee at the end of the war.

Ar 234 Night Fighter

On 4 November 1944 a directive was received from Reichsmarschall Göring for the construction of three prototypes for the night fighter role. The idea of creating an interim two-seat night fighter based on the Ar 234 (comparable to the Me 262 B1a/U1) was conceived in July 1944. In September plans were made to produce 30 Arado night fighters to be converted from standard B-2 production aircraft. The first B-2/N production machine, Werk.Nr. 140146, was supposed to be ready to fly by 19 September 1944, while at the same time plans were being made for series production in Landeshut, Silesia. The first prototype (V1) of the Ar 234 B2/N (now Werk.Nr. 140145) was converted at the beginning of October. Another three prototypes were to be built for the flight test program.

The service trials unit (*Erprobungskommando*) was formed on 12 December 1944 under the command of *Hauptmann* Bisping. The first experimental sorties were flown in early 1945, however no enemy aircraft were shot down.

On 23 February 1945 the commander of the trials unit and his radar operator were killed in the crash of Werk.Nr. 140145.

A new trials unit was subsequently formed on 26 March 1945 under the command of Hptm. Bonow. The interim night fighters flew further sorties from Oranienburg until mid-April 1945. The last serviceable aircraft was ferried to southern Germany after a heavy air raid on Oranienburg. Whether this was the machine at Bad Wörrishofen cannot be determined.

At the end of the war KG 76's last serviceable Ar 234 B-2s were flown to Stavanger in Norway.

One of the few Ar 234 C-3s captured by the Allies.

Test run of the engine of an aircraft of III./KG 76.

1/15 scale model of an Arado Ar 234 C in a realistic forest clearing. The model was built by Günter Sengfelder.

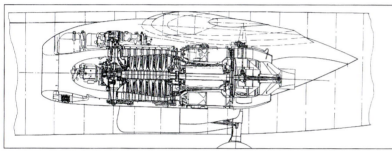

Opposite, Above: Fuselage mock-up with wooden PC 1400.

Opposite, Below: Mock-up with undercarriage down.

Arado 234 C-3 with details of the BMW 003 A power plant, drawn by Günter Sengfelder.

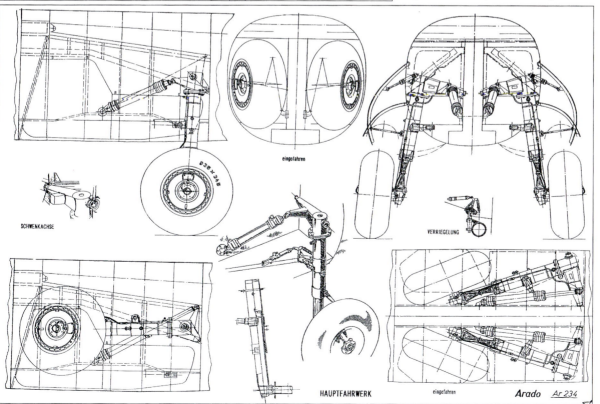

Arado Ar 234 B-2, WerkNr. 140 342, F1 + AS of 8./KG 76 as flown by Obfw. Friedrich Bruchlos in March 1945. This aircraft took part in the attacks on the bridge over the Rhine at Remagen. It is illustrated here carrying a single SC 1000 "Hermann" bomb. Drawing: Manfred Meyer

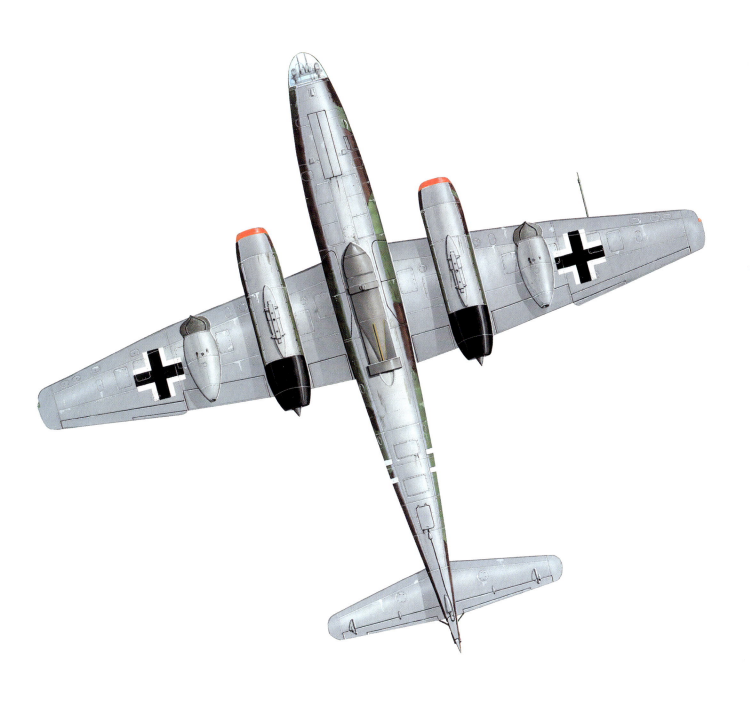

Günter Sengfelder's Arados

Günter Sengfelder is well-known for his scratch-built models in 1/15 scale and has granted us access to his collection of historic *Luftwaffe* aircraft for this publication.

Ar 234 B in a realistic setting, enhanced by scratch-built accessories, also in 1/15 scale.

The revised cockpit section is obvious on this Ar 234 C. With its four turbojet engines this design was a bomber to be taken seriously, one which would have outpaced every Allied fighter. Various developments were planned based on the C-version.

Even an "AWACS" version of the Ar 234 C was planned.

Plans also existed for the C-version to carry a small manned combat aircraft.

The Ar 234 B by Dragon in a realistic setting with *Luftwaffe* tractor.

Ar 234 diorama: the pilot pulls on his jacket in preparation for another mission.

Arado Ar 234 V1 TG + KB on its takeoff trolley, ca. June 1943.

Arado Ar 234 B-2, WerkNr. 140 173 F1 + MT of 9./KG 76. The machine carries a 300-l drop tank beneath each engine nacelle and is finished in a field-applied winter camouflage scheme.

Arado Ar 234 B-2/N "Nachtigall" WerkNr. 140 146, pilot Oblt. Kurt Bonow, radar operator Obfw. Beppo Marchetti, Oranienburg ca. March 1945. The aircraft is equipped with FuG 218 Neptun air-intercept radar and is armed with two MG 151/20 cannon in a pod beneath the fuselage. The lower portion of the cockpit glazing has been painted black to eliminate distracting reflections at night.

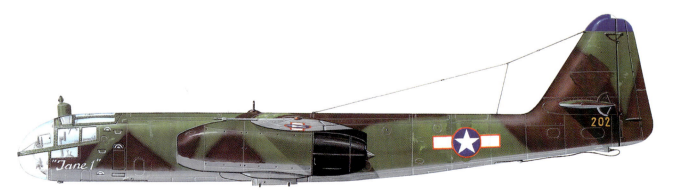

Arado Ar 234 B-2, WerkNr. 140 148, ex F1 + ER of II./KG 76, seen here as it appeared in 1945 as "Jane 1". At that time the aircraft bore the USAAF code 202; it was later passed on to the US Navy, which assigned it the BuAer. No 121445.

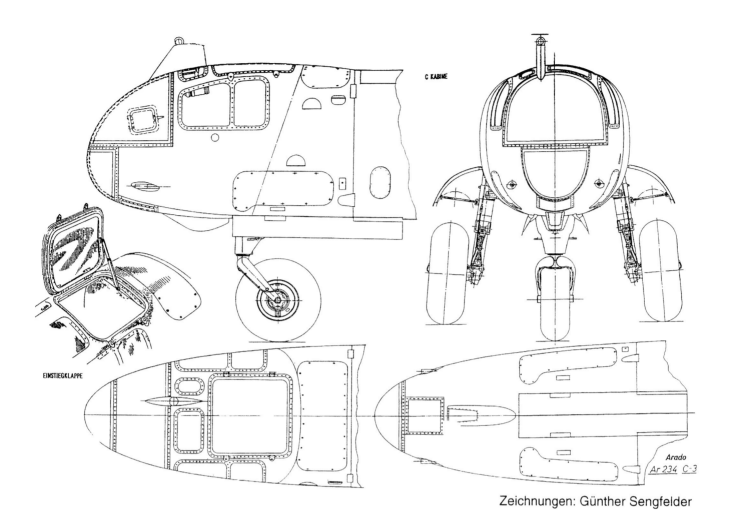

Zeichnungen: Günther Sengfelder

Wire baskets over the engine intakes were supposed to prevent ingestion of debris on makeshift airfields.

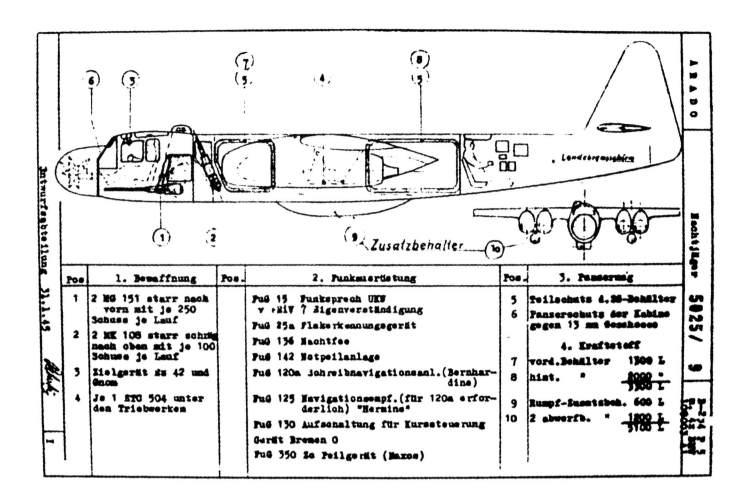
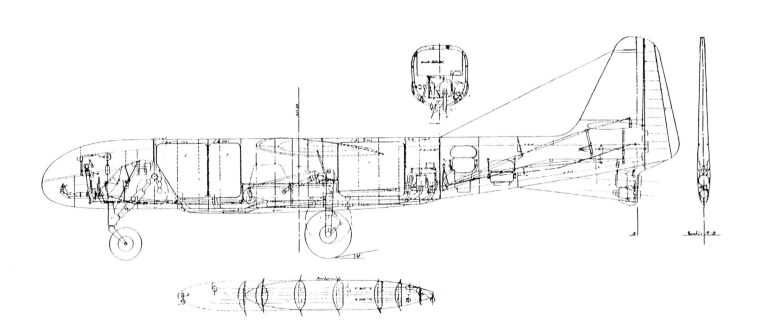

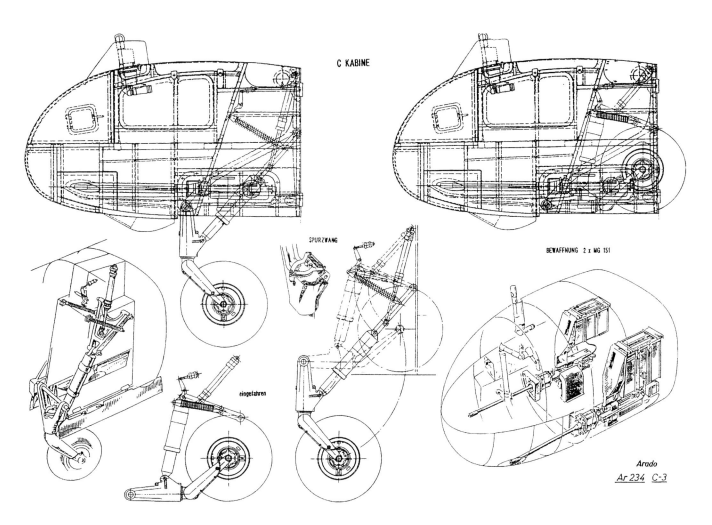

Ar 234 C nose section with armament of two MG 151/20 cannon.

This photo of a Ar 234 reconnaissance aircraft was taken after a crash recovery operation.

TLR / F1 – E2
21/2/45
Situation Report – Ar 234 C

Based on combat experience to date, the Ar 234 C can continue to operate with success. While the Ar 234 C achieves significantly higher speeds, in unit service considerable difficulties can be expected with the four jet engines in the area of operational readiness.

When the E-Stelle examined the Ar 234 C-3 it was found that the expanded radio equipment could not be installed in such a way that the pilot could operate all the systems. Front-line experience has also shown that, given the short mission times, assembling into formation is not possible on account of enemy fighter defenses and fuel consumption. Use of the Lotte sight (horizontal bombing) is therefore not practical. The aircraft bomb with the BZA or the low-altitude bombing system (TSA).

Suggestion:

Continue production of the Ar 234 B, especially since the 004 engine with afterburner (1 150 to 1 200 kg of thrust) will soon be available, resulting in a significant speed for the Ar 234 B, or the quickest possible conversion of the Ar 234 C to accept two HeS 011 turbojets.

1) The performance promised by the company for the 8-234 C was verified:

855 kph at 0 km
880 kph at 2 km
890 kph at 4 km
900 kph at 6 km

2. Course of Development

Overall development of the type may be characterized as normal. There were no major delays resulting from technical difficulties with the airframe or equipment or changes in the type's intended role.

3. State of Development

The type 8-234 C has been replaced as a result of demands for greater performance. At present the V-25 and V-26, which are to be retained by the E-Stelle, are undergoing flight trials or are in the final assembly stage. No serious development work is being done on the C model. Arado is developing a rigid-tow system for increased range.

4. State of Testing

Flight characteristics. Mach problems arise at altitude in level flight (900 kph), making it necessary to restrict speed to 850 kph. For this reason it has not been possible to determine performance at altitude. According to the company, there has as yet been no sign of the expected yaw axis difficulties. Control forces are very sensitive to construction inaccuracies, and smaller tolerances must be prescribed for acceptance.

General. To date only company trials with the V-19 to V-24 prototypes. Approximately 20 test flights have been made at Sagan-Küpper so far. To date testing has been limited exclusively to 109-003 engine trials and Mach difficulties. As well, flight performance, handling qualities, fixed weapons, dropped weapons, undercarriage and pressurized cockpit have been tested to the extent possible.

Airframe

No serious complaints have been registered about the airframe. It was planned to use the V-24 for undercarriage tests (overload takeoffs) at Rechlin. After having been out of service for some time as a result of a taxiing accident, endurance tests could not be initiated because of the B4 fuel shortage. If the reinforced tires do not prove usable, the larger wheel with fuselage bulge will have to be accepted.

Power Plants

Continuous problems because of compressor damage caused by foreign objects, control problems and especially failures of the Riedel starters. As yet there is no data on the broad-based use of J2 fuel. Hot embrittlement of the air-cooled vanes of the compressor wheels of the of the 003 and 004 have resulted in frequent engine failures.

Equipment

a) Radio Equipment. FuG 25a. Equipment had to be moved from the wing to the fuselage. FuG 15 and FuG 25a control units also had to be moved. Operability of the FuG 217 is not assured.

b) Fixed forward-firing weapon. Static firing trial on 9/1/45. Results unsatisfactory. Improvement necessary. Fixed rearward-firing weapon deleted.

c) Bomb-dropping system, preliminary trials with the TSA 2 D on the Ar 234 satisfactory after elimination of minor initial problems

State of Production

a) Ar 234 B-2

188 aircraft have been delivered by the industry as planned. Start-up, which was to have been in February, was delayed by the generally bad transport situation. Instead of 25 aircraft, only about 15 are being delivered in that month. The rest will be delivered in March. There are no difficulties apart from the transport situation mentioned earlier.

b) Ar 234 C-3

February target: 5 aircraft. Start-up was assured. Because of the non-availability of B4 fuel, the installed 109-003 engines had to be removed and replaced with ones converted to use J2 fuel. This is the reason for the delayed start-up. There were also difficulties with the transport of the modified engines.

According to the emergency program (Program Form 24), production is assured for the next 2-3 months.

All Ar 234 C-3s will be delivered ready to use J2 fuel.

The first thirty aircraft will be delivered with the BZA 1B. The requested switch to the TSA II D beginning with the 15th aircraft is not possible, as the installation documents have not yet arrived as of today. It is planned that the BZA 1B system will be replaced by the TSA II D system from the 51st aircraft.

Power plant situation see Situation Report TLR/F1-Rüst. F 2.

1./Versuchsverband d. OKL   H.Q., 13

Mounting takeoff-assist rockets on an operational aircraft of Kommando Sperling.

An Ar 234 B on the runway during takeoff.

An Ar 234 takes off with the help of so-called "Power Eggs."

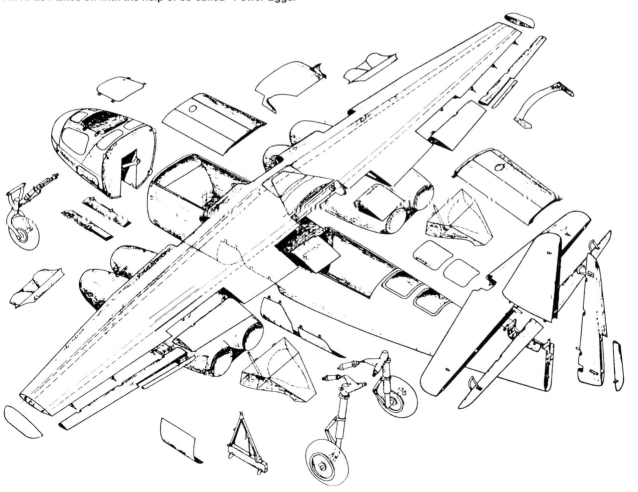

September 1944
Kommando Sperling
Secret

Preparation
By order of the operations staff, the 1./Versuchsverband d. OKL has formed an operational detachment of Ar 234s. On hand are the V5 and V7 powered by the Jumo 004 B with skid undercarriage.

Detachment strength: 2 pilots, 18 technical personnel, 2 civilian airframe fitters and 1 civilian engine fitter. After a brief indoctrination by Arado, on 20 July 1944 the detachment moved to Juvincourt near Reims. Air transport was not authorized, which seriously delayed the arrival of equipment, thus hampering operations. Of the two rail cars carrying special equipment, just one reached the base of operations. As a result of a proposal by the detachment to Luftflotte 3, those replacement parts and special equipment absolutely vital for the immediate commencement of operations were flown in.

Mission Orders
Mission orders from Luftflotte 3 were transmitted to the detachment by way of FAG 123. Weather information was provided by the local meteorological technicians, FAG 123 and Luftflotte 3. Exposed films were immediately turned over to FAG 123 for development and evaluation.

Flight Operations
A FuG 16 was installed on the airfield for the purpose of monitoring landings and takeoffs. During flight operations it was used to maintain contact with another set in the command post which transmitted information on the fighter situation. Sometimes it was also possible to use the Tornado direction-finder on the airfield, which operated on the same frequency. The aircraft were equipped with the FuG 16. The machines were towed to the takeoff point, which took about 20 minutes. After the aircraft took off, waiting trucks moved out to collect the takeoff trolleys and jettisoned takeoff-assist rockets. Two smoke pots were placed on the field to guide the pilot to a landing between the bomb craters, which could not be filled because of the constant state of alert. Hoist, blocks and takeoff trolley were hung on the trucks, ready for use. Time to jack up the aircraft about 30 minutes; total time to return machine to blast pen one hour.

Flight
On all flights the aircraft climbed straight to operational altitude at a speed of 340 – 420 kph on account of the distance from the airfield to the target, remaining below the condensation level if possible. The command post transmitted the enemy situation to the aircraft using the FuG 16. Fighter escort was attempted, but proved unsuccessful. Since the pilots were blind to the rear, above and below, the thirty minutes in the climb were the most vulnerable part of the flight. It was also impossible for the pilot to immediately recognize the formation of condensation trails. In spite of air command advisories, the aircraft were fired on by friendly flak at every airfield. V5 was lost in this way on 28 August 1944.
Total flights by the V5 and V7 by 13 September 1944—familiarization, test, transfer and missions—31, of which 14 were operational sorties.

Technical Findings
In diving flights with the V5 it was found that the upper speed limit is 900 kph at 8 000 meters. At that speed all of the aircraft's control surfaces were ineffective. The V5 demonstrated a tendency to stall in moderately steep turns at 300 kph at low level.

Airframe
The takeoff trolley proved unsuitable for operations, especially from bombed, unimproved airfields. Aircraft were left exposed to enemy action for too long, especially after landing. There were frequent interruptions caused by sagging of the main and support skis, which frequently led to destroyed wingtips. Cockpit heating from jet engines not possible because of exhaust gas.

Power Plants
The engines were operated as gingerly as possible, based on temperature. There have been no failures so far. Total time flown without engine failure V7 approximately 25 hours, V5 approximately 22 hours. Selecting the third jet nozzle position resulted in a speed increase of about 25 kph at 10 000 meters. Difficulties arose in shutting down the engines after a tailwind landing, specifically fires caused by burning of residual fuel. Injection pressure could be maintained to 11 000 meters, no flameouts occurred. Compass failures proved a serious problem which could not be overcome. Readability good at all altitudes, range normal, slight wandering noted after a brief period of operation, receiver could be fine tuned without difficulty.

Cameras
Camera difficulties arose as a result of the mechanism freezing. Misting and icing did not occur, however the forward camera became fouled with hydraulic fluid from the rear main skid strut and overfilling the tank with J2 fuel. This problem was almost completely cured through the installation of deflectors.

Takeoff-Assist Rockets
No rocket failures, only one case of the parachute failing to open, jettisoning was always possible. Rockets proved capable of use up to seven times.

Takeoff Trolley
In one case the trolley failed to release.
Reason: insufficient release travel as a result of release cable being spliced too short and simultaneous pulling out of the electrical release plug and both brake couplings. The aircraft was landed with the trolley in place. The release mechanism was subsequently simplified and replaced with a break point which has functioned perfectly so far. In very case the braking parachute opened and the trolley came to a stop.

Effects of Enemy Action on the Ground
Three times enemy aircraft strafed the machines after they had landed, once the V7 narrowly escaped destruction in a bombing attack. One J2 fuel truck and a wood-gas truck were destroyed.

Transfers
As a result of a lack of transport capacity, the detachment was forced to seek alternate means for the transfers to succeed. No materiel was destroyed or fell into enemy hands. In spite of difficult transfers with the most

Front view of the single-seat bomber version of the C-series (mock-up).

primitive means, in each case the detachment achieved operational readiness immediately after arriving at its new base.

Suggestions
The Ar 234 has proved itself in the western area. Five aircraft with conventional undercarriage are needed for continuous operations and the completion of all assigned tasks. Subsequent machines absolutely must be equipped with FuG 16 ZY and *Erstling*. View to the rear an urgent requirement. External mirror not possible on account of icing, suggest retractable periscope. Furthermore, an attempt should be made to provide heat from the engines for the camera compartment. The possibility of usable cockpit heating should be checked. Serious deviations make the compass unusable, gyro-stabilization is suggested. Installation in the fuselage is probably more favorable. The following equipment is vital for sustained operations as the detachment is completely on its own:

2 tracked vehicles or medium half-track trucks
1 small truck
2 3 _ ton trucks
1 medium motorcycle
3 small motorcycles
2 starter trucks for engine start and radio operation
1 fuel truck for J2

signed Götz.
Oberleutnant and Staffelkapitän

Dies ist ein geheimes Dokument.
Mißbrauch wird bestraft.

Einsatzstaffel III./KG 76
Kommando Hauptmann Lukesch

Kriegstagebuch Nr. 1

Feldpostnummer:	L – 60070	Einsatzhauptort:	Frontfl.St. Quedlinburg
Luftgaupostamt:	Unna		
aufgestellt:	17.12.44	aufgelöst:	26.01.45

Das Kriegstagebuch wurde geführt:
vom: 18.Dez.1944 bis 21.1.1945 durch Oberleutnant Stark

Kriegsschauplatz: Westen

Verluste: Offiziere: 1 Unteroffiziere: ---
         Mannschaften: ---

abgeschlossen.: 26.01.45

Lukesch

(Translation of above)
This is a secret document
Improper use will be punished

Kommando Hauptmann Lukesch

Operational Staffel III./KG 76

War Diary No. 1

Formed:	Quedlinburg 17/12/1944	Disbanded:	26/01/1945
Postal Number:	L – 60070	Opl.Unit:	Frontfl.St.
Air District Post Office:	Unna		

This war diary was maintained:

From: 18 Dec. 1944 to 21 Jan. 1945 by Oberleutnant Stark

Theater of War: West

Casualties: Officers: 1 NCOs: 0
           Enlisted Men: 0

Completed: 26/01/45

Lukesch

Description of Events

On 17 December 1944 the Einsatzstaffel III./Kampfgeschwader 76 with 16 Ar 234 aircraft under the command of Hauptmann Lukesch was formed from 9. Staffel of Kampfgeschwader 76 by order of the General der Kampfflieger on instructions from the *Luftwaffe* High Command (General der Kampfflieger Register of Outgoing Mail number 16610/44 g.Kdos dated 17/12/1944).

On 12 November 1944 the ground elements were transported by rail to the unit's future base at Münster-Handorf. There the necessary ground organization was developed until the *Staffel's* first ten Ar 234 aircraft arrived on 18 December 1944. The remaining six aircraft were ferried from Burg to the base airfield on 24 December 1944.

24/12/1944 Münster-Handorf No missions possible because of weather. *Staffel* 23/12/1944 was ordered to expand the ground organization and technical services.

Mission order see Appendix Volume C, telex 17a 1944 geh.Kdos dated 23/12/1944.

Mock-up of the two-seat Ar 234 cockpit with side-by-side seats.

1st Mission to 1026   **Mission by 9 Arado 234s with takeoff time from 1014 hours.**

Route: Departure base—Iburg beacon low-altitude climb toward Cologne to 4 000 m—approached Liège from out of the sun. Return flight over Cologne or Bonn to home base.
Landing 1122 – 1158 hours.
Attack: Metropolitan areas of Liège and Namur attacked in shallow dive in period 1050 – 1100 hours, attack height 2 000 meters. Nine SC 500 bombs (Trialen) dropped on targeted rail and factory installations and large building complex (city center). Five hits were observed.
Defenses: Weak ground fire from medium anti-aircraft guns was observed. Flights of Spitfires and Thunderbolts were seen in the target area. These took no action, however, as the enemy is probably still unfamiliar with the Ar 234.
Losses: The undercarriage of F1+FT retracted during landing. The wing was damaged. Pilot Uffz. Winguth was not hurt.

2nd Mission   **Mission by 8 Arado 234s with takeoff time from 1452 – 1520 hours.**

Route: same as 1st mission, landing 1600 – 1625 hours.
Attack: Same target was attacked as on the first mission, in a shallow dive in the period from 1531 to 1600 hours. Attack height 4 000 to 2 000 meters. Eight SC 500 (Trialen) bombs were dropped. One SC 500 refused to release and was brought back. None of the pilots saw any strikes on the Liège-North rail station.
Defenses: No ground fire was observed, however there were large formations of bombers and fighters in the target area which had to be flown through, making accurate bombing difficult. No fighter attacks were observed.
Losses: None.
On both missions the route and target were clearly visible and the attack fully accomplished its objective of harassing raid. Both the Liège and Namur rail stations were observed to be full. An airfield housing fighter aircraft was seen north of the city.
Remarks: The operational *Staffel*'s remaining 6 Arado 234s arrived at home base from Burg.

The cockpit mock-up of the Ar 234 C, which was modified several times.

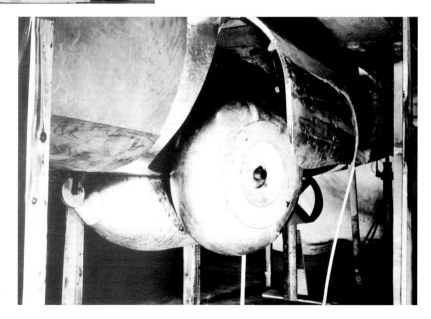

A 1 400-kg store was the Ar 234's maximum possible payload.

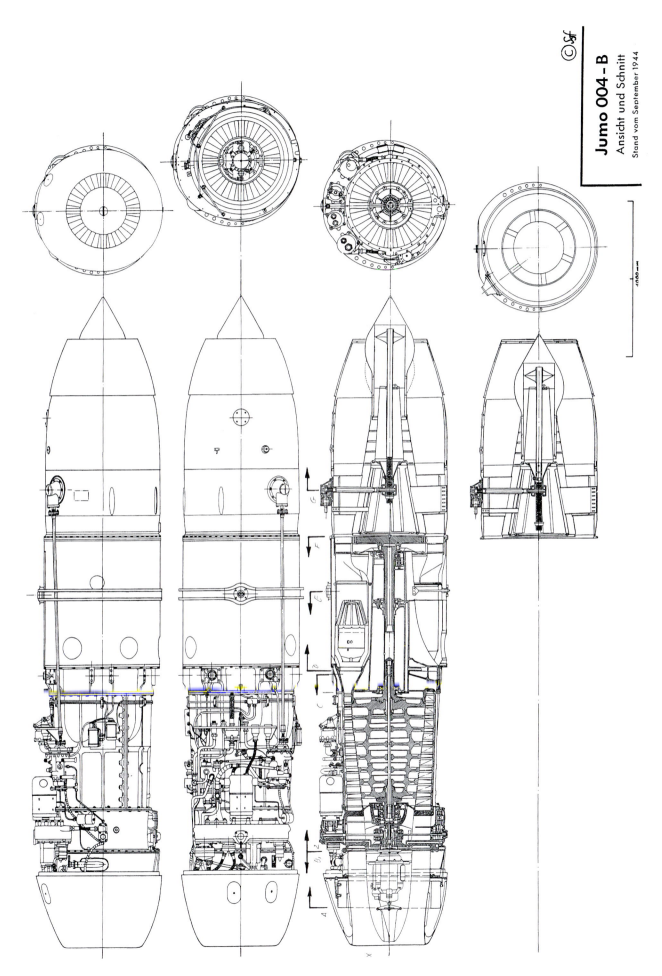

Jumo 004 - B
Ansicht und Schnitt
Stand vom September 1944

Ar 234 A takeoff trolley.

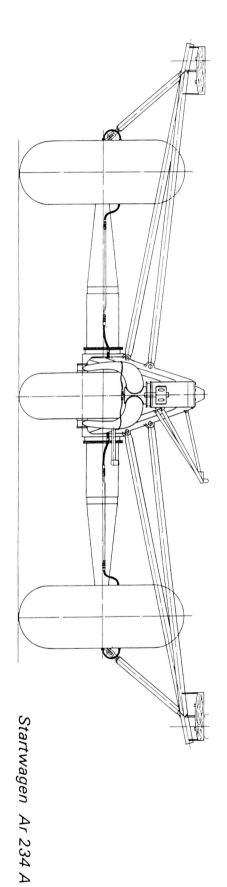
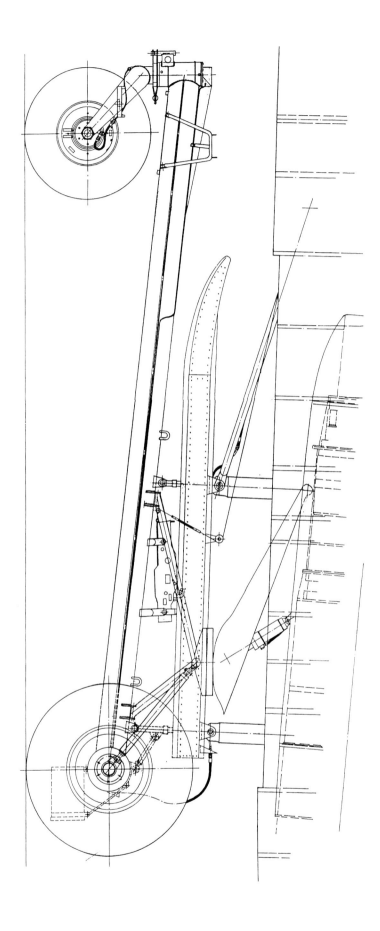

Startwagen Ar 234 A

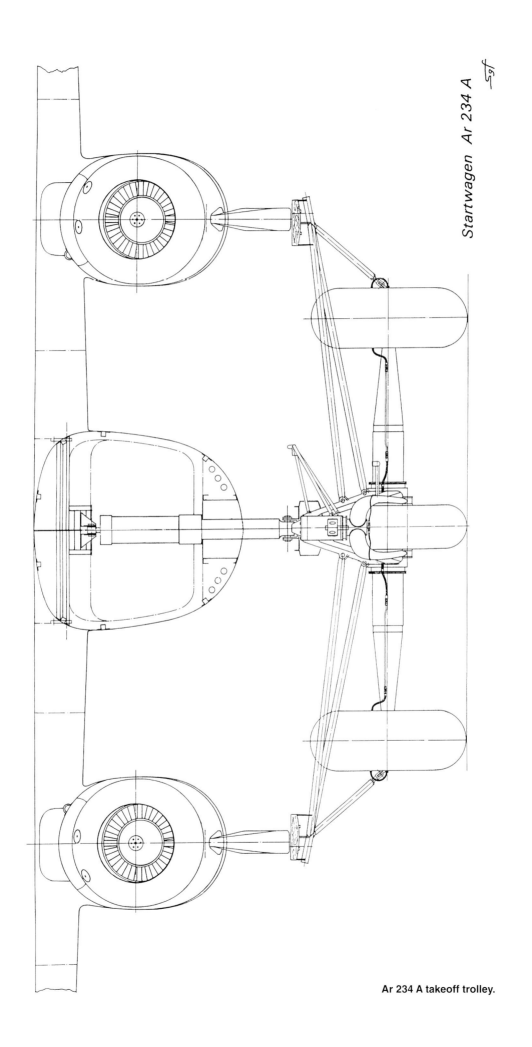

Ar 234 A takeoff trolley.

Ar 234 A takeoff trolley.

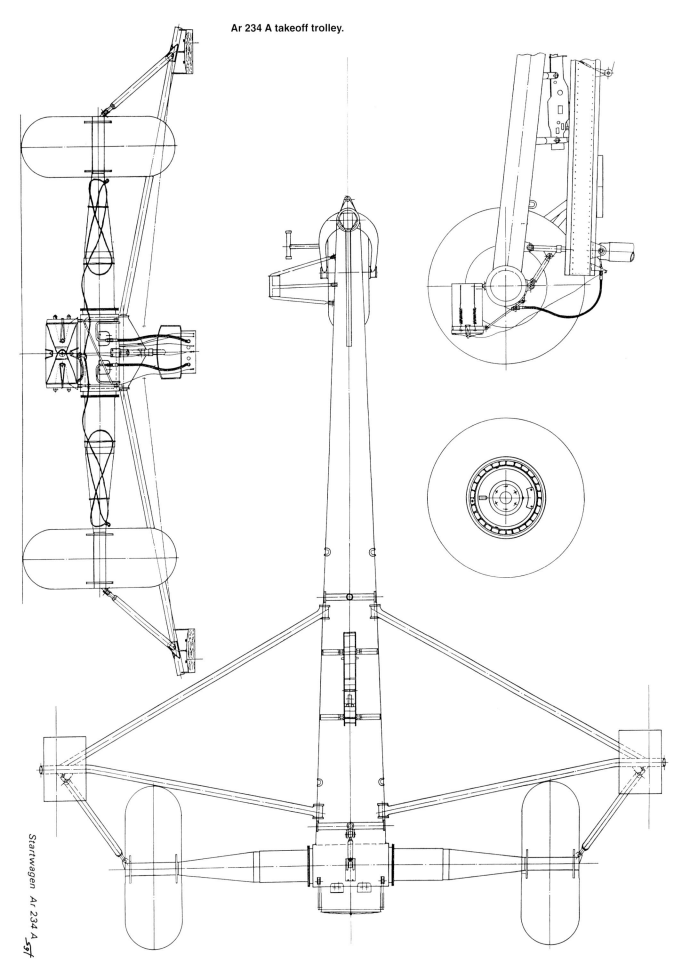

Nosewheel undercarriage member from an Ar 234 crash site prior to restoration.

Right and below left: Two views of the complete undercarriage member after restoration by Günter Sengfelder.

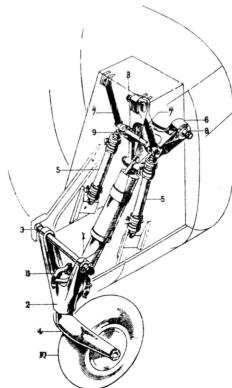

Nosewheel Undercarriage:
1. Shock strut
2. Attachment frame
3. Attachment frame axle
4. Nosewheel fork
5. Nosewheel undercarriage hydraulic cylinder
6. Swivel fitting
7. Shock cylinder
8. Mounting bolts
9. Mounting tube
10. Nosewheel
11. Self-aligner
12.

45

This series of photographs depicts various stages in the construction of a full-size replica of the Ar 234 cockpit by Günter Sengfelder.

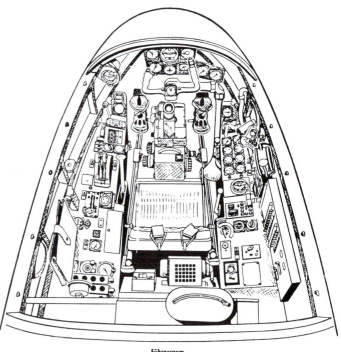

Drawing of the Ar 234's cockpit.

Left: Interior shot of the beautifully-restored Ar 234 B in the USA.

1/15 scale model of an Arado Ar 234 B by Günter Sengfelder.

Arado Ar 234 C in 1/15 scale. This model is also part of the Sengfelder collection.

Diorama with Ar 234 C from the Sengfelder collection. Photo by Robert Kroeschel.